This book is dedicated to all the quick brown foxes who compelled to jump over the backs of countless lazy dogs.

We are forever in your debt.

Also to Ceela, Sophie and Luke the Alpha Dog.

My First Book of Fonts: A Garden of Typographical Verse

Written and illustrated by Kevin Glasgow

ISBN: 9798343339598

©2024. All rights reserved.

This book was created on a MacBook Pro using the Adobe Creative Cloud software suite, primarily Adobe Illustrator, and Adobe InDesign.

All typefaces used in the production of this book are licensed through their respective agencies.

A is for Arial,

Helvetica's replicant

(though shaped a little rounder

with terminals aslant).

Like all grotesks, it's serif-free,

quite readable and neat.

Just like a little mermaid,

this face is without feet.

ẞ is for Bauhaus,

a geometric jewel

of typographic excellence

named for the German school.

Since circles, squares and triangles

define the Bauhaus style,

its simple shapes and angles

should delight the typophile.

C is for Clarendon,

a face that's just the tonic

for when you're in a classic mood

and feel a bit Ionic.

Its slab serifs are bold and strong

without looking too solemn.

And like its architectural kin,

it looks good in a column.

D is for Dom Casual.

He's never in a rush

He's loose and free and looks like he

Just dripped from the end of a brush.

Dom hails from the age of the painted sign

That's why he's so informal

And while that might seem odd to some

For Dom it's all quite normal.

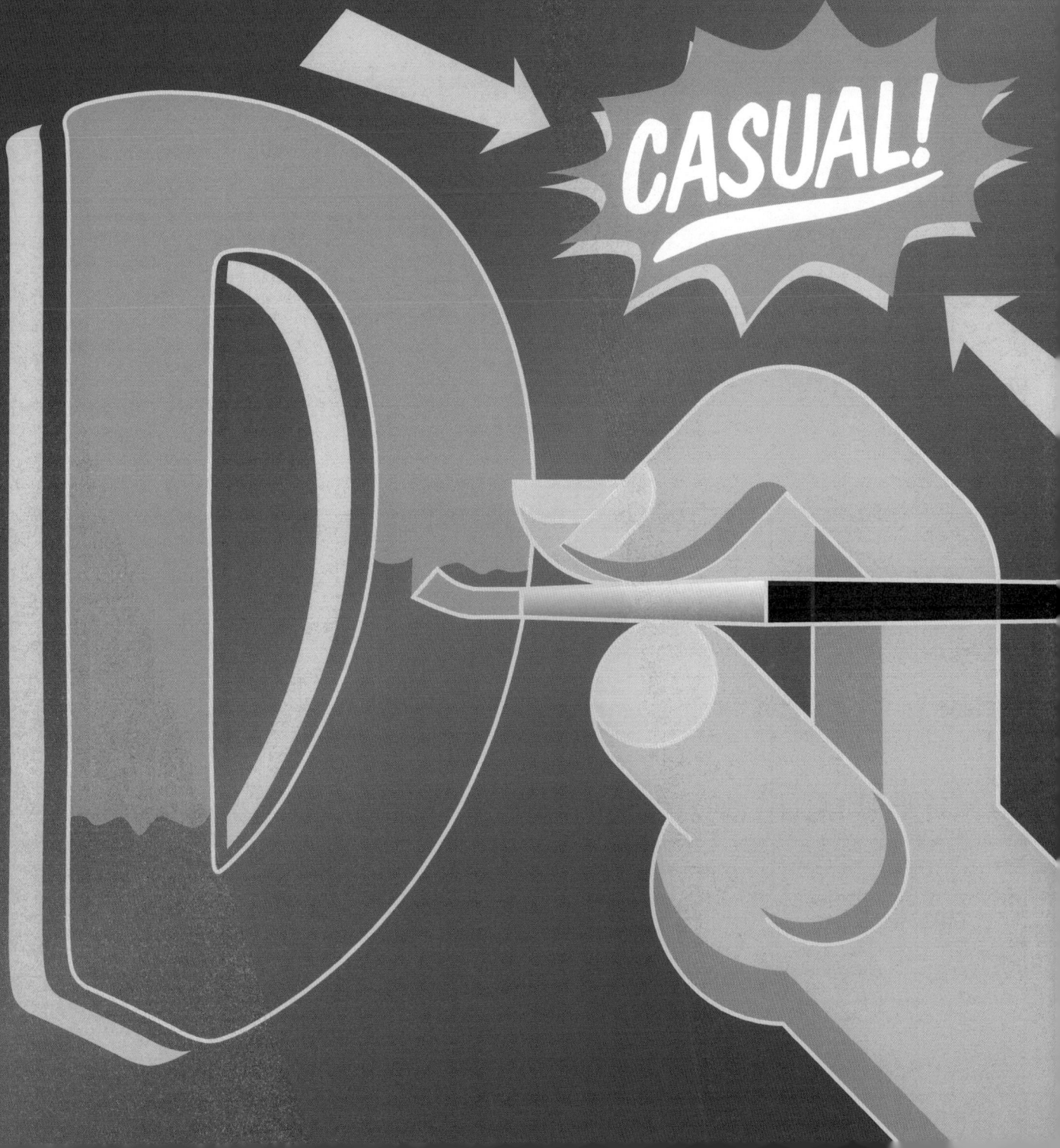

E is for Eurostile,

a futuristic face

for spaceships or computers

or any high-tech place.

Both round and square at the same time,

like an old TV screen.

Could that be why it looms so large

on the science fiction scene?

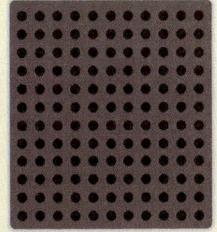

F is for Futura,

Paul Renner's great endeavor.

Its shapes are geometric

(which really is quite clever)!

And if you're keen on trivia,

here's a fact to make you swoon:

Futura's the first typeface

left by men upon the moon!

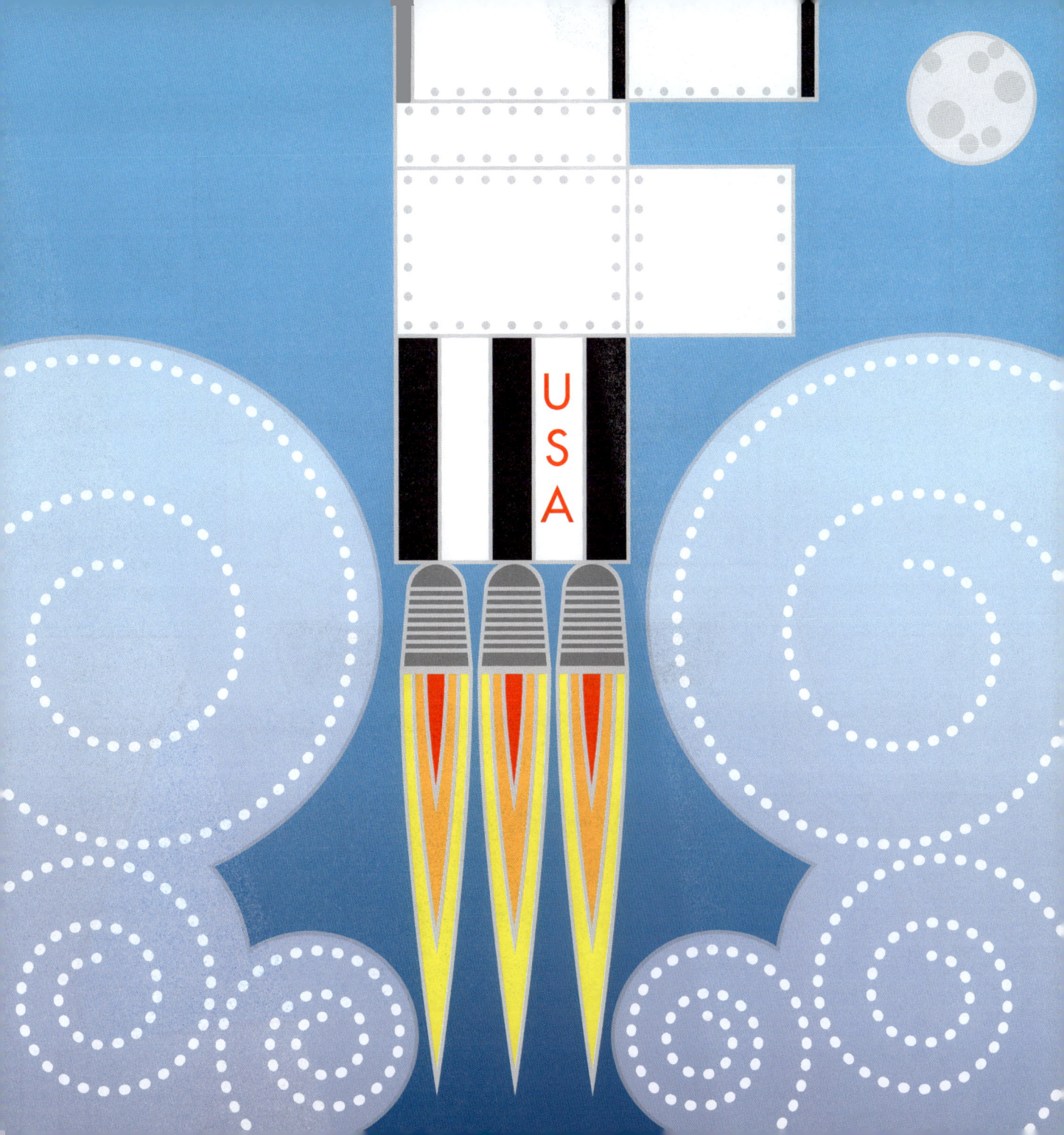

USA

G is for Gill Sans,

a gem by any measure.

The king of type! The type of kings!

A humanistic treasure!

When you can't find a typeface

that will suit your design plans,

don't lose your head. Like Churchill said,

"Keep calm and use Gill Sans!"

KEEP CALM
AND USE
GILL SANS

POWER

TH
NERVE C
OF LON

UNDER

H is for Hobo,

Mo Benton's vagabond.

An Art Nouveau-ish artifact

from an era now long gone.

It languished oh so many years,

a typographic relic,

until the hippies dug it up

and turned it psychedelic.

I is for Impact,
ubiquitous, it seems,
as the internet's preferred typeface
to grace a thousand memes.
It's big and bold and bossy
to grab online attention.
But is that outline needed
to improve our comprehension?

J is for Jenson,

named for the pioneer

who left his home in Paris

for a Venetian atmosphere.

His fondness for the Roman form

no doubt made reading better.

If not for him, you'd have to read

this book in all Blackletter!

K is for Kabel,

a German geometric.

Circles paired with sharp straight lines,

it's simple, yet majestic.

Created by a master,

Herr Rudolf Koch by name.

Germany was his passion

and typography his game!

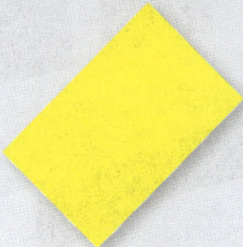

FREE KERNING

ECKMANN AVENUE

AND?

WEISS WAY

BAUER FOUNDRY

RENNER ROAD

HELLBOX

BERNHARD ROAD

GO TO MAINZ

SPIEKERMANN STREET

HELLBOX

TSCCICHOLD PLACE

BERTHOLD FOUNDRY

BELWE BOULEVARD

AND?

BAUM DRIVE

WOLPE WAY

AND?

ZAPF AVENUE

STEMPEL FOUNDRY

BAUER BOULEVARD

HELLBOX

GUTENBERG WAY

JUST IN CASE SORTING

AICHER PLACE

HELLBOX

WILKE WAY

KLINGSPOR FOUNDRY

PANNARTZ PLACE

AND?

SWEYNHEIM STREET

L IS FOR LITHOS,

EVOKING ANCIENT GREECE,

OLYMPUS AND THE PARTHENON

AND GOOD OLD PERICLES.

IT HAS AN ERSATZ SENSE OF SOME

HELLENIC HISTORY.

AND WHILE THAT MIGHT MAKE SENSE YOU,

IT'S STILL ALL GREEK TO ME.

M is for Mistral,

a script that's magnifique!

Elegant and expressive,

One might even say, "Trés chic!"

But if you set this in all caps

I'll tell you, "C'est dommage!"

(Plus, letterspacing script

is typographic sabotage!)

M

Parfum de Paris

N is for News Gothic,

a vestige from an age

when news was spread around the world

upon the printed page.

When deadlines loomed for headlines!

And type was metal-cast!

Are newspapers and magazines

just relics of the past?

O is for Optima,

a balanced, serene sans.

A treasure for the eye to see

such letters drawn by hand.

Flexible and nimble

and quite easily read.

Like yoga, it's quite useful for

both the body and the head.

P is for Papyrus,

which evokes antiquity,

approximating age with its

rough-edged calligraphy.

The typolitterati

will deride it in their chorus.

But who's to judge? Perhaps we'll take

the matter up with Horus.

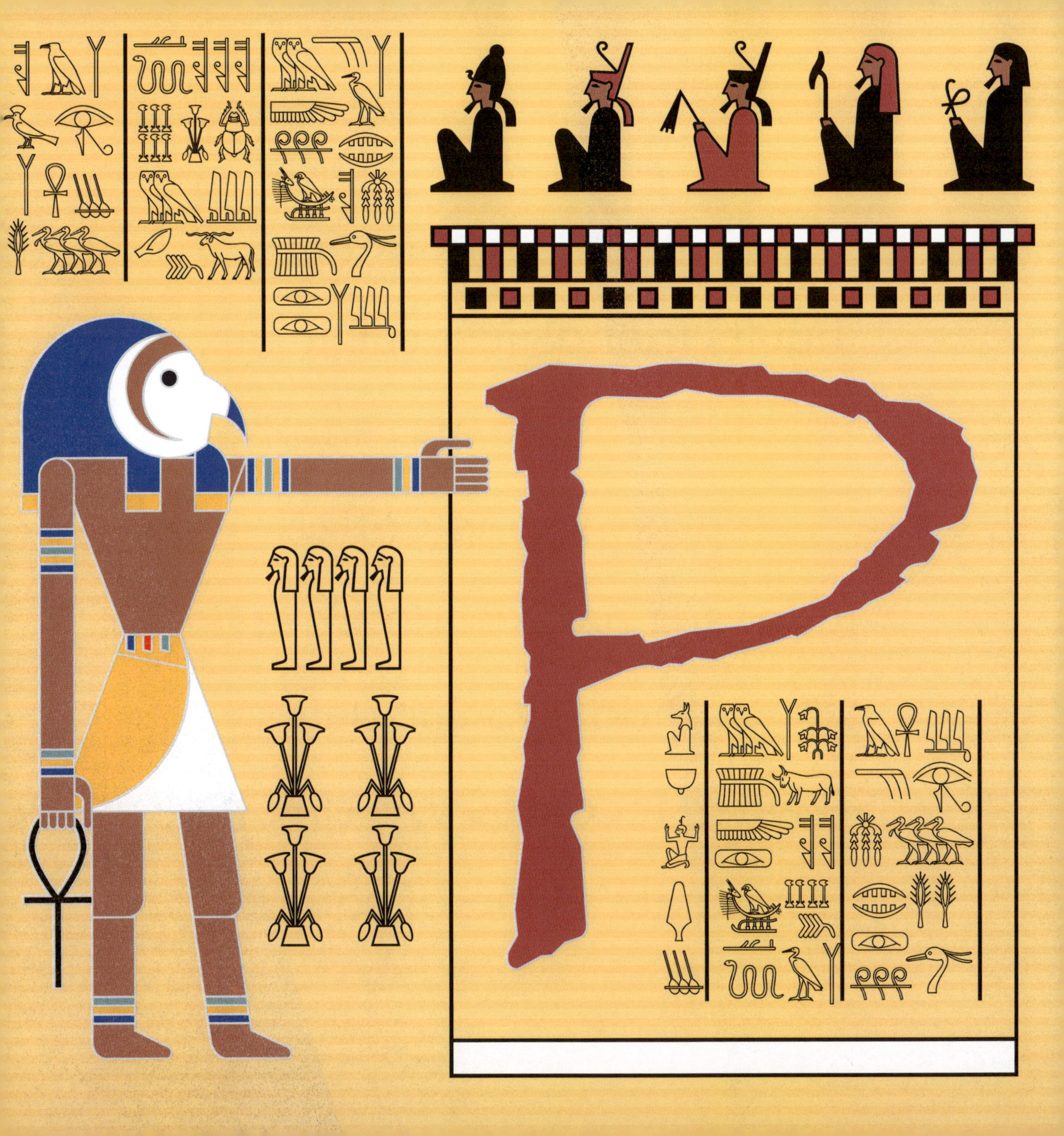
P

Q is for Quadrata,

but its friends just call it Friz.

It's quite sedate and somber.

It doesn't pop or fizz.

It doesn't have Bodoni's style

or Didot's Gallic flair.

So when it comes to being hip,

Quadrata's kind of square.

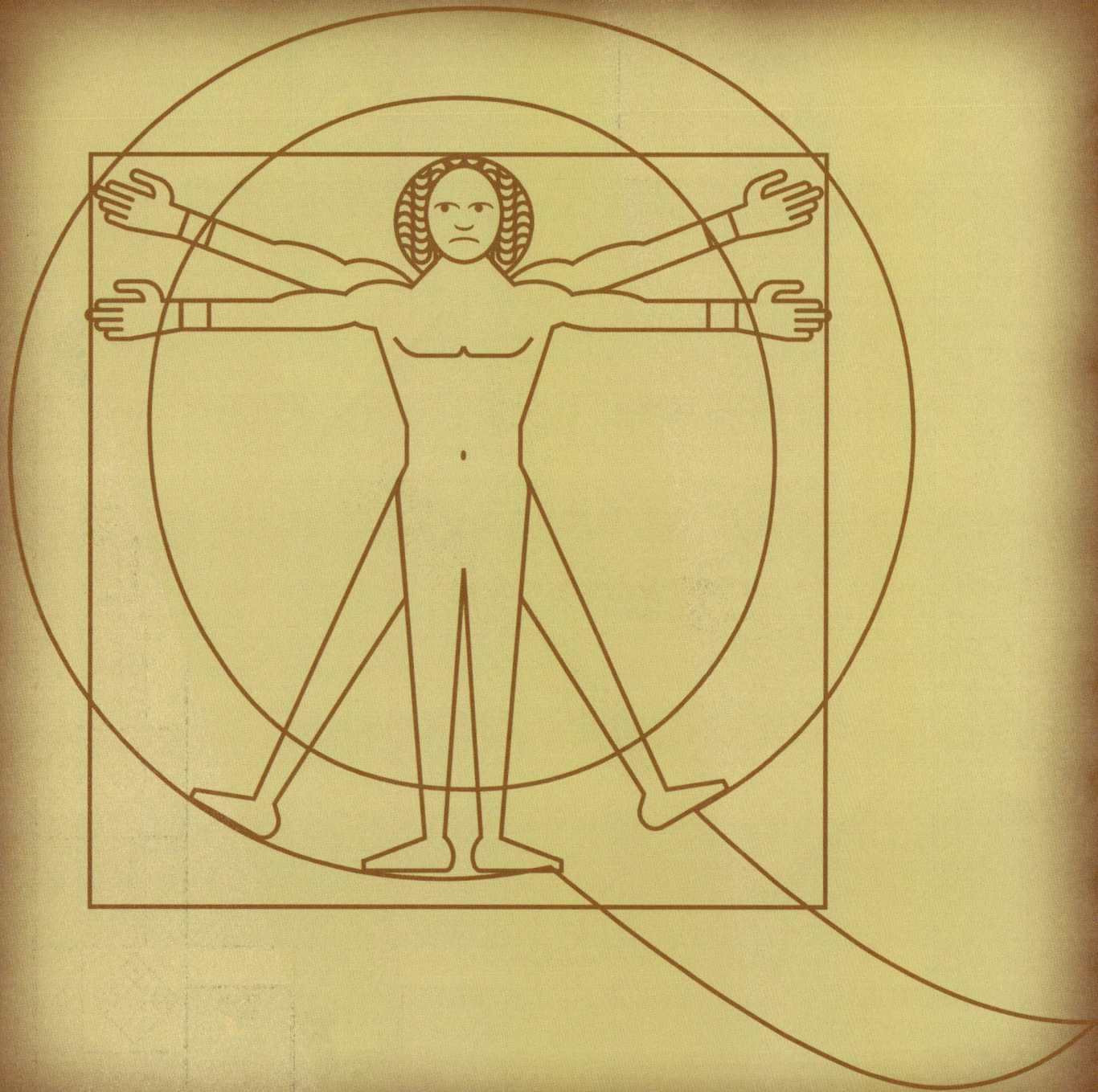

R IS FOR ROSEWOOD,

WHICH NEEDS LITTLE EXPLANATION:

POLYCHROMATIC LETTERS WITH

EXCESSIVE ORNAMENTATION!

A THROWBACK TO THE WILD WEST DAYS

OF USING WOODEN TYPE

FOR POSTERS, BANNERS AND DISPLAYS

IN ADVERTISING HYPE!

S is for Souvenir,

a mild-mannered sort.

For any typographic task,

he's happy to report!

What's in the sky? A bird? A plane?

The ghost of Oswald Cooper?

No need to fear, it's Souvenir!

A type that's simply super!

T is for Trajan,

That famous font you know.

It's seen on movie posters.

It's seen in TV shows.

No minuscule is needed

when your look is so imperial.

So if you seek a lower case,

you're not Trajan material!

CELEBRE LITTERAE

SENATVSPOPVLVSQVEROMANVS
IMPCAESARIDIVINERVAEFNERVAE
TRAIANOAVGGERMDACICOPONTIF
MAXIMOTRIBPOTXVIIIMPVICOSVIPP
ADDECLARANDVMQVANTAEALTITVDINIS
MONSETLOCVSTANTISOPERIBVSSITEGESTVS

U is for Univers,

a superfamily font.

Italic, Roman, **thick** or thin,

it's everything you'd want.

Every *style* and **weight** is there

to meet your text's demands.

While other fonts have limits,

our Univers **expands.**

V is for Verdana,

made for computer screens.

A face that's quite familiar

to both commoners and queens.

It's sans-serif, it's humanist,

but it has few fawning fans.

Perhaps that's why when it grows up,

it wants to be Gill Sans.

W is for Windsor,

a rather British name

for a rather British typeface

that's earned rather British fame.

It's rather good in titles

or in headlines or that lot.

But if you're setting body text,

Windsor rathers that you not.

FURARI PROHIBERE OVIS

X is for X-Height,

a term of type construction,

like crossbar, bracket, stem and spur,

used in a font's production.

Shoulder, spine, ear, tail and eye

are important parts of text!

(I can't recall a typeface

that begins with letter X!)

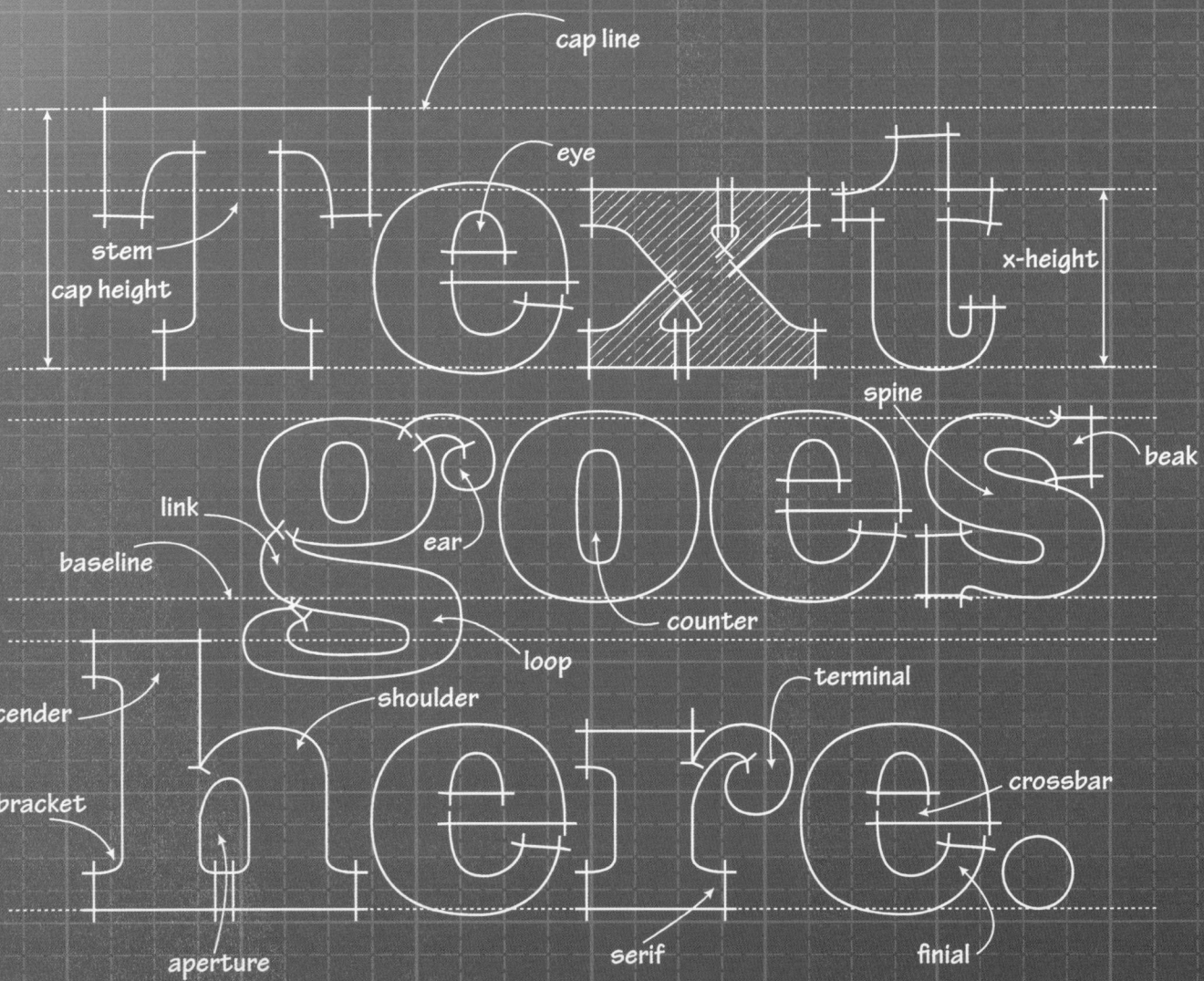

Text goes here.

cap line

eye

stem

cap height

x-height

spine

beak

link

baseline

ear

counter

loop

ascender

shoulder

terminal

bracket

crossbar

aperture

serif

finial

TYPOGRAPHY CONSTRUCTION	
Project #	A113
Client	Fust & Schoeffer
Supervisor	J. Gutenberg

Y is for Yale,

a proprietary face

designed by Matthew Carter

for New Haven's learning place.

A lovely, classic Roman style,

Refined to the last detail.

But you and I can't use it,

because Yale is not for sale!

Z is for *Zapfino*,

a calligraphic wonder!

With ascenders that fly like flags

as descenders dive down under.

So please don't diss this lovely script

by the master, Hermann Zapf.

To set it in all caps would be

a typographic gaffe!

Typefaces used in this book

Arial
Year: 1982
Designers: Robin Nicholas, Patricia Saunders
Foundry: Monotype

ITC Bauhaus
Year: 1975
Designers: Ed Benguiat, Victor Caruso
Foundry: International Typeface Corporation

Clarendon
Year: 1845
Designer: Robert Besley
Foundry: Fann Street Foundry

Dom Casual
Year: 1951
Designer: Peter Dom
Foundry: American Type Founders

Eurostile
Year: 1962
Designer: Aldo Novarese
Foundry: Nebiolo

Futura
Year: 1927
Designer: Paul Renner
Foundry: Bauer

Gill Sans
Year: 1926
Designer: Eric Gill
Foundry: Monotype

Hobo
Year: 1910
Designer: Morris Fuller Benton
Foundry: American Type Founders

Impact
Year: 1965
Designer: Geoffrey Lee
Foundry: Stephenson Blake

Adobe Jenson
Year: 1989
Designer: Robert Slimbach
Foundry: Adobe
Based on the works of printer and typographer Nicolas Jenson, generally regarded as the creator of one of the earliest Roman typefaces.

Neue Kabel
Year: 2016
Designer: Mark Schütz (after Rudolf Koch)
Foundry: Linotype
Neue Kabel is a revival of Kabel, originally designed by calligrapher Rudolf Koch and released by the Klingspor Foundry in 1927.

Lithos
Year: 1989
Designer: Carol Twombley
Foundry: Adobe

Mistral
Year: 1953
Designer: Roger Excoffon
Foundry: Fonderie Olive

News Gothic
Year: 1908
Designer: Morris Fuller Benton
Foundry: American Type Founders

Optima
Year: 1958
Designer: Hermann Zapf
Foundry: D. Stempel

Papyrus
Year: 1982
Designer: Chris Costello
Foundry: Letraset

Friz Quadrata
Year: 1965
Designers: Ernst Friz and Victor Caruso
Foundry: Visual Graphics Corporation

ROSEWOOD
Year: 1994
Designers: Carl Crossgrove, Carol Twombley,
Kim Buker Chansler
Foundry: Adobe

ITC Souvenir
Year: 1971
Designer: Ed Benguiat
ITC Souvenir is a revival of a classic typeface first
designed by Morris Fuller Benton in 1914 for
American Type Founders.
Foundry: International Typeface Corporation

TRAJAN PRO
Year: 1989
Designers: Carol Twombley, Robert Slimbach
Foundry: Adobe

Univers
Year: 1957
Designer: Adrian Frutiger
Foundry: Deberny & Peignot

Verdana
Year: 1996
Designer: Matthew Carter
Foundry: Microsoft

Windsor
Year: 1905
Designer: Eleisha Pechley
Foundry: Stephenson Blake

Tekton Pro
Year: 1989
Designer: David Siegel
Foundry: Adobe

ITC Galliard Pro
Year: 1978
Designer: Matthew Carter
Foundries: Linotype, International Typeface
Corporation

Zapfino
Year: 1998
Designer: Hermann Zapf
Foundry: Linotype

Printed in Great Britain
by Amazon